YOUR KNOWLEDGE HAS VALUE

Moritz Wenninger

Nationalparks - Anfänge und Erbe der Natur

GRIN Verlag

Bibliografische Information der Deutschen Nationalbibliothek:

Die Deutsche Bibliothek verzeichnet diese Publikation in der Deutschen National-
bibliografie; detaillierte bibliografische Daten sind im Internet über http://dnb.d-
nb.de/ abrufbar.

Imprint:

Copyright © 2011 GRIN Verlag GmbH
Druck und Bindung: Books on Demand GmbH, Norderstedt Germany
ISBN: 978-3-656-30552-1

This book at GRIN:

http://www.grin.com/en/e-book/201869/nationalparks-anfaenge-und-erbe-der-
natur

GRIN - Your knowledge has value

Der GRIN Verlag publiziert seit 1998 wissenschaftliche Arbeiten von Studenten, Hochschullehrern und anderen Akademikern als eBook und gedrucktes Buch. Die Verlagswebsite www.grin.com ist die ideale Plattform zur Veröffentlichung von Hausarbeiten, Abschlussarbeiten, wissenschaftlichen Aufsätzen, Dissertationen und Fachbüchern.

Visit us on the internet:

http://www.grin.com/

http://www.facebook.com/grincom

http://www.twitter.com/grin_com

Index:

According to the US government agency, the percentage of visitors of National Parks keeps rising continuously every year, for example in 2009, there was a total amount of 285 million persons in the US parks, an increase of about 3,9 percent in comparison to the year 2008.[1]

What are the reasons for tourists travelling sometimes hundreds of miles just to visit one of those places?

John Muir, a naturalist and pioneer spokesman for the National Parks in 1898 already used the following words:

> *"Thousands of tired, nerve-shaken, over-civilized people are beginning to find out that going to the mountains is going home; that wilderness is a necessity; and that mountain parks and reservations are useful not only as fountains of timber and irrigating rivers, but as fountains of life."* [2]

Even nowadays, or better to say especially nowadays a rising stress rate among people can be noticed[3], and as a result of this development, more and more people are seeking for little paradises – the National and State Parks – to enjoy a little time out in the unspoilt and untouched wilderness during their free time or holidays.

An amount of uncountable National Parks extends all over the world, the USA itself contains 58 official National Parks at the moment.[4] Millions of humans enjoy this priceless legacy every year, but few stop to think about the source of this bounty.

What is the background of these parks, why and when were they founded?

Which expections can be fulfilled by National Parks?

In the following, these questions will be answered while giving you – the reader of this research paper - a new point of view on nature and especially evolving and reminding you of the breathtaking scenery of National Parks in the USA and worldwide.

---

1 http://www.n-tv.de/reise/Great-Smoky-Mountains-vorn-article748593.html
2 Krell D.: National Parks of the West, California: Lane Publishing Co. 1988, p.10
3 http://www.dasdiabetesblog.de/wohlstandsdiabetes-eine-modekrankheit-der-heutigen-gesellschaft/
4 http://de.wikipedia.org/wiki/Nationalparks_in_den_Vereinigten_Staaten

1. Definition and Comparison: National and State Parks

First of all, it is to be clarified what a National Park or State Park actually is and in which ways they differ.

National and State Parks serve similar purposes, they preserve a certain area of landscape. The differences between these two kinds of parks are only nuances, but they may lead to confusion among the visitors.

Basically, National Parks denote areas which have some kind of national interest, as the name says, for example the Grand Canyon National Park.

In contrast to National Parks, State Parks highlight areas of statewide interest such as Fall Heritage State Park in Massachusetts.

Many State Parks charge an entrance fee - as National Parks also often do - and offer annual park passes, for people intending to visit a special park regularly. Such passes vary from stickers, that can be placed on a vehicle, up to cards, which are shown to staff upon entering the park.

State Parks are usually under the direction of the Department of Natural Resources or conservation for the particular state you would like to visit.

" (...) [T]he Department of Interior has basic responsibility for water, fish, wildlife, mineral, land, park, and recreational resources. Indian and Territorial affairs are other major concerns of America's Department of Natural Resources. The Department works to assure the wisest choice in managing all our resources so each will make its full contribution to a better United States – now and in future."[5]

Most national parks are administered by the National Park Service.[6] [7]

Emblem of the National Park Service, stands at the entrance of each national park

5   Linn R. M.: Research in the Parks, Library of Congress Cataloging in Publication Data, p. iv
6   http://www.associatedcontent.com/article/1825641/state_parks_vs_national_parks_what.html?cat=16
7   Sky Worell G.: Faszinierendes Amerika Alle National-Parks der USA, Bindlach: Gondrom Verlag 1994, p. 29

Jean-Paul Harroy gave a definition of what a park should be, that was accepted by IUCN (International Union for Conservation of Nature) in its General Assembly in New Dheli in the year 1969:

> "A national park is or should be: (1) a relatively large area; (2) where one or several ecosystems are not materially altered by human exploitation and occupation; (3) where plant and animal species, geomorphological sites, and habitats are of special scientific, educational, and recreational interest or which contains a natural landscape of great beauty; (4) where the highest competent authority of the country has taken steps to prevent or eliminate as soon as possible exploitation or occupation in the whole area and to enforce effectively the respect of ecological, geomorphological, or esthetic features which have led to its establishment; and (5) where visitors are allowed to enter, under special conditions, for inspirational, educational, cultural, and recreational purposes."[8]

Furthermore, governments are requested to exclude from the above definition: areas that are scientific reserves which can only be entered by a special permission; nor a natural reserve, that is managed by a private institution without competent authority of the state; nor an inhabited and exploited area where landscape planning and measures are taken. At least a minimum size, adequate staffing and a certain budget is required for maintenance and protection of a park.[9]

Arranged in 1933 during the London Convention and the 1940 Washington Convention, hunting or capturing of flora and fauna is strictly forbidden.

Neither Germany's nor Great Britain's National Parks fit these criteria as they are being used for a variety of purposes including settlements and agriculture.[10] To sum it up, most of the National Parks do not only serve for the protection of flora and fauna, but also for the outdoor leisure of people. Furthermore such an experience of nature can contribute to the personal attitude towards nature conservation in a positive way. Therefore it is an ambitious task for the National Park Service to balance on the one hand the preservation of nature's goods and on the other hand the public accessibility to such goods.

---

8   Dasmann R. F.: Research in the Parks, Library of Congress Cataloging in Publication Data, p. 2
9   Ibid., p. 2
10 Ibid., p. 3

2. The National Park History

The idea of preserving chosen sceneries goes back to the early 19th century when the American painter George Catlin in 1832, claimed this movement.[11] While travelling through the wilderness, painting and drwaing portraits, landscapes and also scenes from daily Indian life, he worried about the preservation of all this beauty that surrounded him, as well as the culture of the Native Americans.[12]

His idea was to create special areas, set aside from normal development, where the natural grandeur as well as the lands of the Native American could be preserved.

Although in the 1830's no move was taken by the federal government in this sort of direction, the idea of creating grand parks to preserve the natural beauty of the country slowly began to gain acceptance. In 1864, first steps towards creating a national park were set in motion by Congress and President Abraham Lincoln.

It was for the first time ever, when in 1864 under President Abraham Lincoln, an area of Yosemite Valley finally was set aside for the pleasure of all humans. This was the political spark which initiated the founding of the first National Park at the Yellowstone River in the year 1872 – the Yellowstone National Park. This was the year of Catlin's death, having lived with the dream to see first steps towards a National Park.

John Muir accomplished the enlargement of further reservations in California during the year 1890. He was the founder of the Sierra Club, which was lead by him for 22 years and that is nowadays one of the most influental nature conservation association.

Thirteen years later in 1903, John Muir said to US president Theodore Roosevelt, who was talking about hunting as a freetime activity he would never understand these issues, if he couldn't get over this meaningless killing.[13] The president, actually a friend of nature, had to admit that Muir was right and agreed to camp outside in

11 http://de.wikipedia.org/wiki/Nationalpark
12 http://de.wikipedia.org/wiki/George_Catlin
13 http://www.waidlerherz.de/geschichte_nationalparkidee.pdf

the wilderness of Yosemite for four days.  The photograph depicts President Thedore Roosevelt and John Muir standing on Glacier Point in Yosemite. As a result of this meeting, Roosevelt returned to Washington determined to expand the protection of nation's scenic, historic and natural heritage.[14]

During his legislative period, among other things, three National Parks were founded which extend over a several million acres.

That is the reason for Muir being described as father of the American National Park System. All National Parks were founded in the stunning scenery of the West until 1919, as the first National Park, the Acadia National Park, was established in the East of the USA.

About 1200 land owners were forced to give up their rural farms located in the park area, mostly because of the global economic crisis.

In addition some wealthy citizens donated countryside for public reservations and for maintenance of the Wild America.

Far away from protecting all kinds of animals in the parks was the National Park Service (NPS), founded in 1916 under the umbrella of the Department of the Interior, prosecuting the extinction of unpopular carnivores such as wolves, pumas and coyotes with the help of fire arms. Insects were killed by an insecticide called DDT, and natural forest fires were stopped. Streets and hotels were built, just to satisfy the demands of a rising amount of visitors, because relaxation of people was sadly more important than the recovery of nature.

John R. White described the situation at this time:

> "*There is a natural and steady pressure to place amusement and entertainment above other requirements. In many national parks the interests of local visitors conflict with those of national visitors and with the preservation of the park for the future.*"[15]

14 Krell D.: National Parks of the West, California: Lane Publishing Co. 1988, p.12
15 White J.R.: America's National Park System the critical Documents, Rowman & Littlefield Publishers 1994, p.143

Only now in 1935, after the extinction of wolves in the Yellowstone National Park, people began to realize what a mistake had been made as the population of wapitis and buffalos exploded, due to missing natural enemies, which of course wolves had been.

This is a complex system and if the human interrupts such a system, it will get out of control and as a consequence, a huge amount of wapitis and buffalos had to be shot down. In 1960 the great wapiti slaughter was in the press nearly everywhere and three years later, an article of the zoologist A. Starker Leopold was published in which he postulated that each park should be a copy of the primitive untouched America, in the way the first Europeans explored it. During the same year a study of the National Academy appeared, that described the parks as complex systems of nature and an invaluable source for science. Rachel Carson, a marine biologist warned that the use of chemical pesticides would have an adverse effect on the ecosystem.

Though they were used since 1966, consisting of EDB (Ethylene-dibromide) mixed with diesel oil. By now, nature was moving into foreground and not people's pleasure. Then, a natural forest fire destroyed about 40% of the Yellowstone National Park in 1988.

According to scientists, the park was biologically ready for the fire as former ones were averted by humans, therefore park administration has acted in the right way, as they preferentially saved the buildings.

Following with the Vail-Report in 1991, some proposals were suggested to the National Park Service, that had the aim to balance tourism and conservation. One of these steps was the reintroduction of wolves – against the opposition of residents and farmers - into the ecological system of Yellowstone in 1995, on the grounds that wolves had been a species of the original Yellowstone and were needed for the natural regulation of wapitis for example.[16]

---

16 http://www.waidlerherz.de/geschichte_nationalparkidee.pdf

2.1 America's Best Idea

Not for nothing this development during the centuries is called America's Best Idea. Americans were the first people who founded the first National Park, the Yellowstone National Park in 1872 and initially even used the army for protection of the park till 1916.

With people talking about this great idea nowadays, they mean exactly this idea, having its origin in the USA, that was such a brilliant one, with the consequence of spreading all over the world.

Writer and historian Wallace Stegner described National Parks as:

> "[T]he best idea we ever had. Absolutely American, absolutely democratic, they reflect us at our best rather than our worst." [17]

Another person, Ken Burns, a filmmaker and honorary National Park ranger, tells the story of National Parks and the people who created them in his movie, of course called ` The National Parks: America's Best Idea´.[18]

There is also a book existing being titled with the same name, containing a lot of spectacular pictures of parks, which can be viewed on the internet.[19]

2.2 The Idea around the World

The best idea went around the world and finally reached Europe with founding the first National Park being located in Graubünden, Switzerland in 1914. National Park leader Dr. Schloeth compared the essence of a National Park to a room of a house, through which visitors can watch, without inhabitants noticing.

It is obvious to see the parallels between the above exemplification and the basic American idea of a park. Attendants are only guests, who are allowed to come inside and have a look at all the beauty, nature presents, but have to leave parks in their original status.[20]

---

17 http://www.nps.gov/americasbestidea/
18 Ibid.
19 http://www.americasbestidea.com/
20 http://www.waidlerherz.de/geschichte_nationalparkidee.pdf

The first National Park being established in Germany was the Bayerischer Wald in 1969. In the former GDR, National Parks were not requested due to political reasons, although about 15% of the country's area was not accessible for public and therefore almost offered untouched nature. Before the reunion of Germany, five National Parks had been established in the GDR untill 1989.[21]

The main idea behind National Parks in Germany is equally the preservation of countrysides with a special characteristic for example a rare geological appereance or endangered species.

Germany contains 14 National Parks at the moment, that make up 0,54% not counting the marine district, of Germany's land area.

Compared to other countries in Europe, this account is quite amiss, as Czech Republic and Austria provide about 3% of space for National Parks.[22] Only three of the 14 National Parks fit to IUCN criteria, which were defined by this organisation by order of UNO.

At least 75% of so called ` Kernzone´ is required to attain the name National Park according to IUCN standarts.

` Kernzone´ describes the zone where there is nothing else than nature, no farming and no humans regulating for example populations of parasites. Most of Germany's National Parks do not reach these 75% as the following graphic shows:[23]

Nr.	Nationalpark	Gründungsjahr	Gesamtfläche (ha)	IUCN-Anerkennung
I	Bayerischer Wald + Erweiterung	1970/1997	13042+10800	Ja
II	Berchtesgaden	1978	21000	Ja
III	Schleswig-Holsteinisches Wattenmeer	1985	285000	Nein
IV	Niedersächsisches Wattenmeer	1986	240000	Nein
V	Hamburgisches Wattenmeer	1990	11700	Nein
VI	Vorpommersche Boddenlandschaft	1990	80500	Nein
VII	Jasmund	1990	3000	Ja
VIII	Müritz-Nationalpark	1990	31800	Nein
IX	Hochharz	1990	5868	Nein
X	Sächsische Schweiz	1990	9292	Nein
XI	Harz	1994	15800	Nein
XII	Unteres Odertal	1995	22400	Nein
XIII	Hainich	1997	7600	Nein
XIV	Elbtalaue	1998	10500	Nein [23]

Quelle: Bundesamt für Naturschutz/eigene Recherche

21 http://www.uni-protokolle.de/Lexikon/Nationalpark.html
22 http://de.wikipedia.org/wiki/Nationalparks_in_Deutschland#cite_note-0
23 http://www.nabu-akademie.de/berichte/98NATPARK.htm

By the year 2002, ` Bundesnaturschutzgesetz´ defined the aim of National Parks to assure biological cycle in its natural dynamic.[24] Humans should not interfere in this cycle, they have to learn that even catastrophes like floodings and wind blast belong to this natural dynamic of nature.

Around the world there is a total amount of 2041 National Parks existing now – depending on the way of definition - with 180 of them located in Europe.[25]

3. Parks around the World

3.1 USA – Yellowstone National Park

This park is the flagship of the National Park Service and of course the oldest one. Its name comes from the Yellowstone river, which is the most important in the whole park. But first of all some data about the park in general:

" * World's First National Park
* 2,219,789 acres (Larger than Rhode Island and Delaware combined)
* Wildlife - 7 species of ungulates (bison, moose, elk, pronghorn), 2 species of bear and 67 other mammals, 322 species of birds, 16 species of fish and of course the gray wolf.
* Plants - There are over 1,100 species of native plants, more than 200 species of exotic plants and over 400 species of thermopholes.
* Geology - The park is home to one of the world's largest calderas with over 10,000 thermal features and more than 300 geysers. It has one of the world's largest petrifiied forests. It has over 290 waterfalls with the 308' Lower Falls of the Yellowstone River as it's showpiece.
* Yellowstone Lake is the largest (132 sq. mi.) high altitude (7,732') lake in north america.
* 9 visitor centers
* 12 campgrounds (over 2,000 campsites) " [26]

The park is located in Wyoming, West USA. Yellowstone is also home to a huge vulcano, the Yellowstone – Volcano. Its magma chamber, which lies 8 kilometers below soil surface, is so enormous that this volcano is

[27]

24 http://www.waidlerherz.de/geschichte_nationalparkidee.pdf
25 http://www.nabu-akademie.de/berichte/98NATPARK.htm
26 http://www.yellowstonenationalpark.com/

the biggest in the whole USA.[27] Native Americans have lived in the Yellowstone region for at least 11,000 years, just to mention one of the reasons why it is necessary to preserve this landscape. Because it is part of American history. The park is also famous for its stunning geysers as one of the largest – the Old Faithful – lies among 300 others in the park. It erupts approximately every 91 minutes.[28]

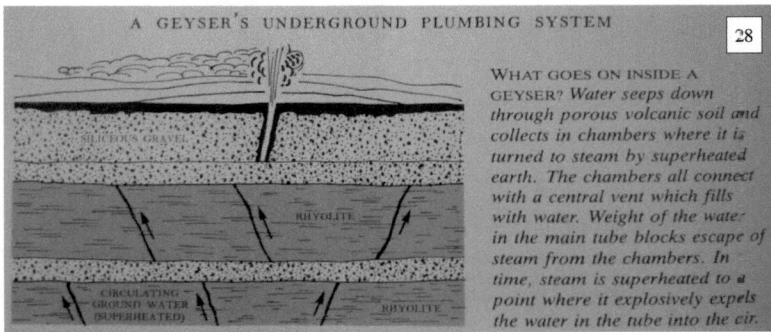

A GEYSER'S UNDERGROUND PLUMBING SYSTEM [28]

WHAT GOES ON INSIDE A GEYSER? *Water seeps down through porous volcanic soil and collects in chambers where it is turned to steam by superheated earth. The chambers all connect with a central vent which fills with water. Weight of the water in the main tube blocks escape of steam from the chambers. In time, steam is superheated to a point where it explosively expels the water in the tube into the air.*

To implement the idea of a wild and untouched nature in its original status, wolves were reintroduced as lots of them were shot down to nearly extinction in former times.

On the one hand it should be mentioned that these wolves belong to nature and have an impressive character, but on the other hand one has to keep in mind that wolves are carnivores and so visitors should keep enough distance to them. The same counts for bears and bisons.

Such a National Park is a paradise for itself, but comes along with few negative aspects, for example ranchers being concerned about large bison populations, that could transmit diseases to their domestic cousines. In fact, there is no real need to worry, because this case never happened.

27 http://de.wikipedia.org/wiki/Yellowstone-Nationalpark
28 Krell D.: National Parks of the West, California: Lane Publishing Co. 1988, p.204

To draw a conclusion, Yellowstone National Park is for sure worth a visit, if you obey a few rules you can experience nature in a way you never did before, in its pure beauty, which will grab your attention within few minutes.[29] [30]

3.2 Germany – National Park Bayerischer Wald

National Park Bayerischer Wald, of course in Bavaria, was the first National Park which was established in Germany in 1970, almost 100 years later after the first one was founded in the USA.

The park itself lies in the Bayerischer Wald and makes up 243 km², compared to almost 9000 km² of the Yellowstone National Park, it is rather tiny, but one has to mention, that Germany is not as big as the USA.[31] Together with the bordering Czech Böhmerwald, Bayerische Wald forms the greatest woodland area in Central Europe. Most of the area is stamped by former forestry, but nowadays no one interrupts these forests – in ` Kernzone´ - anymore, even catastrophes are no longer averted, as they belong to the original circle of nature. The most momentous mountain in the park is the ` Große Rachel´ which is 1453 meters high, besides this attraction a lot of moors can be visited, which are just one concern of the park's preservation. The park is not only needed for protection of nature, but also as economic factor, with 700.000 people visiting Bayerischer Wald every year.[32]

---

29 http://de.wikipedia.org/wiki/Yellowstone-Nationalpark
30 http://grandcanyon.free.fr/images/cascade/original/Colors,%20Lower%20Falls,%20Yellowstone %20National%20Park.jpg
31 http://www.bayerischer-wald.de/urlaubsthemen-/natur-erleben/nationalpark/
32 http://de.wikipedia.org/wiki/Nationalpark_Bayerischer_Wald

Just as well as in American National Parks, many rare animals have been saved from extinction in German National Parks, for example Lynxes, wolves and sometimes one can even watch an elk. The last lynxes had died out in 1850, and finally 120 years later were reintroduced. The population began to grow very fast, but during the 90's this population decreased rapidly because of illegal shootings mostly in the Czech Republic. Another typical inhabitant of the park is the red deer, which stays in a huge gate during the winter months to avert damage caused by game animals on trees.[33] Another parallel between German and American parks can be found: wolves in general are dangerous animals if one gets close to such an animal, therefore visitors have to be attentive and unfortunately some wolves broke out of their gate in 2002 so that there was a real danger existent. At the beginning rangers were confident to catch the wolves without killing them, but later on as only one of the wolves had been caught, shootings were considered, as a bullet of a gun can pass much longer distances than one out of a narcosis gun could. In the end the remaining wolves outside of the gate were shot as rangers saw no other possibility to catch them. According to some naturalists, not the human has to fear the wolf, but the wolf has to fear the humans and people should learn to respect nature and creatures that seem to be strange, instead of killing them.[34]

In the ` Kerngebieten´ - the areas of Kernzone – it is not allowed to leave routes, dogs must be leashed, camping is possible in designated areas, and of course no one is allowed to take things like plants or animals home, to mention some behavioral rules.[35]

Heated discussion came along with the escape of a bear at the German – Austrian border, that had to be shot down, by reason of failed tries to catch the bear alive. [36]

---

33 http://de.wikipedia.org/wiki/Nationalpark_Bayerischer_Wald
34 http://www.abschaffung-der-
   jagd.de/informationen/forschungtexteartikel/woelfeimbayerischenwald/index.html
35 http://de.wikipedia.org/wiki/Nationalpark_Bayerischer_Wald
36 http://www.spiegel.de/panorama/0,1518,423537,00.html

Here one has to mention, that a bear is more dangerous than a wolf, but many environmentalists judged this shooting as irresponsible.
Youth organisations of ` Bund Naturschutz´ talked about a tragedy of Bavarian nature preservation. It is for sure sad in its way, but rangers had to balance reasons and the bear was not killed immediately, contrariwise even special bear hunters were brought to Germany, who tried to catch the bear with the help of trained dogs, but without success.[37]

Bayerischer Wald is a popular place in Germany and should be visited during a trip to Germany in every case.
Offering a wide range of freetime activities from mountaineering to walking in the woods and skiing, everyone's pleasure is guaranteed.[38]

3.3 Great Britain – Lake District National Park

In Great Britain one can find almost the same amount of National Parks than in Germany, to be precise one more than in Germany, 15, of which 10 are located in England, 3 in Wales and 2 in Scotland. The first three National Parks were founded in the year 1951, so a bit earlier than in Germany.

There is no park in Ireland, however efforts are made to establish one in near future.[39]

37 http://www.spiegel.de/panorama/0,1518,423537,00.html
38 http://lotgdforum.de/members/kiterou-albums-natur-picture2762-bayrischer-wald.jpg
39 http://de.wikipedia.org/wiki/Nationalparks_im_Vereinigten_K%C3%B6nigreich

The parks cover about 7%of land's area, that is almost 14 times more than in Germany. In contrast to other countries, National Parks in Great Britain are not administered by the state. Each park is managed by its own National Park agency. That is why a lot of space of the parks is under private property. Estimated 110 million people visit the parks yearly.[40]

Lake District is known for its spectacular landscape of lakes and mountains and lies in Cumbria, Northwest England. It covers an area of 2172 km² and is 130 kilometers away from Manchester.

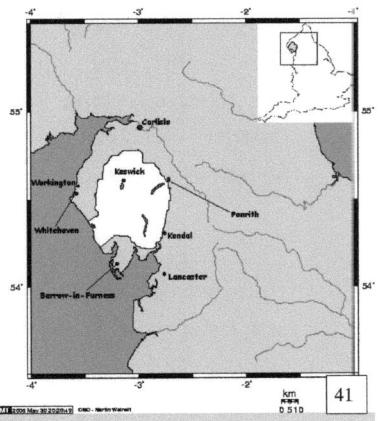
41

The area became popular because of William Wordsworth, a poet and friend of nature, who dedicated some of his literature to the Lakes and therefore is called a ` Lake Poet´ .

Important economic aspects are tourism of course and sheep breeding.

Lake District is a result of many ice ages which created the lakes by ice melting 15.000 years ago.

The park shelters the only golden eagle pair of England, and also the last European squirrels that were suppressed by the North Amercian squirrel on the rest of the island.

Environment Agency enacted a new law to protect rare species of fish, in which is said that fishermen are no longer allowed to use fish as decoys. Mainly during the 16th till 19th century, mining was the main economy in Lake Destrict. Graphite was digged in huge amounts so that a whole pencil industry grew up there.

Nowadays tourism is the main economic sector.[41]

40 http://de.wikipedia.org/wiki/Nationalparks_im_Vereinigten_K%C3%B6nigreich
41 http://de.wikipedia.org/wiki/Lake_District

The fotograph depicts Scafell mountain, with 978 meters altitude, the highest in Lake District. If you are in Great Britain and not far away from Manchester, you should not miss attending Lake Destrict – because you will  be attired in just as the ` Lake Poets´ once were.[42]

4. Conclusion and Future Prospects

Today we can look back on a history of National Parks, that started off with its success in the United States of America and spread all over the world. Humans began to realize that nature is mother of all life on earth and donates everything we need to live, but demands our protection.

With the step of establishing National Parks all over the world, we made one little movement towards this aim, but a lot of work needs to be done in future, as more and more questions come up about global warming or deforestation. Personally I can only repeat the words of John Muir, nature is home, and wilderness is a necessity as it is the fountain of life. Everyone can contribute to a better environment, just by using their bike for example, if everyone did such little things, we would have a better world in general. Rainforests are described as the lung of the earth, what will happen, if we destroy our own lung on earth? Without being able to breathe, life will disappear. To demonstrate that this topic, especially about National Parks, is still up to date, a newspaper article can be found in the addendum, that deals with the topic of a new National Park in Germany – the Steigerwald.[43] Furthermore you can find two videos in addendum, that give you an impression of parks in America and opinions of people about them.

42 http://de.wikipedia.org/wiki/Lake_District
43 Lösung für den Steigerwald from Fränkischer Tag, on 11. December, p.14

Resources:

Internet:

http://www.abschaffung-der-
jagd.de/informationen/forschungtexteartikel/woelfeimbayerischenwald/index.html

http://www.americasbestidea.com/

http://www.associatedcontent.com/article/1825641/state_parks_vs_national_parks_wha
t.html?cat=16

http://www.bayerischer-wald.de/urlaubsthemen-/natur-erleben/nationalpark/

http://www.dasdiabetesblog.de/wohlstandsdiabetes-eine-modekrankheit-der-heutigen-
gesellschaft/

http://grandcanyon.free.fr/images/cascade/original/Colors,%20Lower%20Falls,
%20Yellowstone%20National%20Park.jpg

http://lotgdforum.de/members/kiterou-albums-natur-picture2762-bayrischer-wald.jpg

http://www.nabu-akademie.de/berichte/98NATPARK.htm

http://www.nps.gov/americasbestidea/

http://www.n-tv.de/reise/Great-Smoky-Mountains-vorn-article748593.html

http://www.spiegel.de/panorama/0,1518,423537,00.html

http://www.uni-protokolle.de/Lexikon/Nationalpark.html

http://www.waidlerherz.de/geschichte_nationalparkidee.pdf

http://de.wikipedia.org/wiki/Lake_District

http://de.wikipedia.org/wiki/Nationalpark

http://de.wikipedia.org/wiki/Nationalpark_Bayerischer_Wald

http://de.wikipedia.org/wiki/Nationalparks_im_Vereinigten_K%C3%B6nigreich

http://de.wikipedia.org/wiki/Nationalparks_in_den_Vereinigten_Staaten

http://de.wikipedia.org/wiki/Nationalparks_in_Deutschland#cite_note-0

http://de.wikipedia.org/wiki/Yellowstone-Nationalpark

http://www.yellowstonenationalpark.com/

Print Media:

- Dasmann R. F.: Research in the Parks, Library of Congress Cataloging in Publication Data
- Krell D.: National Parks of the West, California: Lane Publishing Co. 1988
- Linn R. M.: Research in the Parks, Library of Congress Cataloging in Publication Data
- Lösung für den Steigerwald from Fränkischer Tag, on 11. December
- Sky Worell G.: Faszinierendes Amerika Alle National-Parks der USA, Bindlach: Gondrom Verlag 1994
- White J.R.: America's National Park System the critical Documents, Rowman & Littlefield Publishers 1994